How to Meditate without attending a TM class

*Akins/
Nurnberg*

AMJON

EASY STEP BY STEP INSTRUCTIONS PLUS FREQUENTLY ASKED QUESTIONS AND THEIR ANSWERS!

How to Meditate without

INCLUDING INSTRUCTIONS FOR SELECTING A PERSONAL MANTRA.

attending a TM class

by W.R. Akins and H. George Nurnberg, M.D.

Distributed by
Crown Publishers, Inc.
New York

Distributed by Crown Publishers, Inc.

MANUFACTURED IN THE UNITED STATES OF AMERICA
First Printing

Akins, W. R.
    How to meditate without attending a TM class.

    Bibliography: p.
        1. Meditation. 2. Transcendental Meditation.
I. Nurnberg, H. George, joint author. II. Title
BL627.A35   131'.32   76-2995
ISBN 0-517-52636-0

CONTENTS

FOREWORD

Meditation is practiced by large numbers of people, perhaps more than one million in this country alone. This recent trend indicates that a need of vast numbers of people can be met by the use of this technique. The reduction of tension and anxiety is clearly at this focus. Though tension, pressure, and anxiety are associated with modern times, man has been seeking to control these feelings since the beginning of his existence. Drugs and alcohol have too frequently been uséd as the modalities of escape, only to create an even heightened level of tension and vast human misery. Meditation offers a "new" (though actively old) method, whereby the individual himself, under his own power, is able to have an impact on this unpleasant emotional state. It is the mastery of this noxious condition which offers the potential of heightened self-awareness and self-fulfillment.

The deleterious effects of longstanding tension and anxiety are well known to the medical profession. Psychiatrists and other mental health professionals have long seen the interrelationship between emotional illness and anxiety as a primary focus of attention. A great number of physical illnesses are now known to be influenced by emotional factors. Most of the major organ systems of the body (skin, respiratory, cardiovascular, nervous, intestinal, etc.) have clearly been demonstrated to be responsive to tension and anxiety in negative ways. For more favorable outcomes of treatment and more importantly, for prevention of illnesses, modern medicine is aware of the need for patients to be as free of tension as possible. Tension control offers the possibility of preventing or reducing the extent of morbidity in many illnesses. Prevention is clearly the most efficient way to deal with problems. Meditation may well offer benefits beyond those of increased well-being through prevention.

Meditation is clearly not an end in itself or the answer to all the world's problems. However, it can be effectively utilized as a positive experience that may well help an individual more closely reach his potential and even achieve a condition he never thought himself able to. To be certain, it will not substitute for a doctor when actually ill, a friend when alone, or a job when unemployed, but it may help an individual who wants to help himself achieve those things more efficiently.

H. George Nurnberg, M.D.
Assistant Professor of Psychiatry
The New York Hospital
Cornell Medical Center

Publisher's Note

Many books have been published on the subject of meditation, particularly Transcendental Meditation (TM). Some of them have even appeared on the bestseller lists. Unfortunately, the most popular "TM books" inadvertently implied, or at least held out the hope, that they would teach the reader exactly how to meditate. They did not. These books were, in effect, "long-playing advertisements" for TM class enrollment and hundreds of thousands of book buyers felt cheated.

The readers of this book will not be disappointed. They will learn exactly HOW TO MEDITATE WITHOUT ATTENDING A TM CLASS since we sincerely believe that anyone who can read, can meditate. It's that simple.

S.A.M.

INTRODUCTORY NOTE

This book is an invitation to the reader to discover his or her "meditation potential." It is also an attempt to take the mystery out of this highly controversial subject.

Specifically, this book will provide an introduction to, and instruction in, the transcendental meditation technique. It will also offer an alternative form of meditation, one that, for many people, works as well as does TM (Transcendental Meditation).

Since this is a controversial area, I want to say first, that I am not an "official" teacher of TM and, consequently, this book is not biased by any professional obligations to the TM organization. The author has found that TM does work for him although there are several criticisms made regarding the TM movement. I hope that my points of disagreements will be clear to the reader, just as I hope they are fair to the TM movement.

To begin with, the ease and effectiveness of the TM technique surprised me, although I had often heard that people began to derive benefit from it almost immediately. It also became clear to me why, in these high-pressure and energy-depleting. times, meditation, especially the TM method, has become "big business." (It is estimated that

TM enrollments are now running at the rate of approximately 30,000 students per month . . . and growing rapidly!)

This statistic is not offered as a "put-down" of the TM movement, but rather as a means of underscoring its deserved popularity. The TM technique is, in effect, a product designed to satisfy a human need. Best of all, it's a product that really works. Like most good products, TM will continue to grow and prosper as long as it continues to work and fill a need—and as long as people are able to "pay the price."

If you are one of those who can afford the $125 for the TM course and live reasonably close to a teaching center, I strongly urge that you attend and receive your instruction there. You will most likely benefit from the discipline and personal exchange involved in any type of school environment. But what of those who can not, or will not, meet all the course requirements . . . obviously there must be millions? For them, this book is a logical alternative.

The leaders of the TM movement state, and rightly so, that "anyone who can think, can meditate." They are dedicated to making TM available to everyone, stating that, if only one per cent of the world's population were to practice TM, the quality of life would improve and mankind would achieve its ultimate good. However, until everyone can meet the current financial and other requirements of the TM course, their goal of world-wide meditation and enlightenment is obviously impossible. It is hoped that this book, in its own way, will help to bring the TM goal closer to fulfillment.

Considering that subjects far more complicated than the TM technique have been successfully taught through books, the author can truthfully say that had this book been available, it would have enabled him to meditate as effectively as he is doing today.

Therefore, this book is dedicated to the premise that "anyone who can read, can now meditate," and to the enrichment and improvement of life for all individuals, whether or not they are able to afford personal paid instruction.

CHAPTER ONE

An Advance into the Primitive

It has become a commonplace observation that the social revolution of the Sixties has become the mystical revolution of
the Seventies. Never has the youth of the
nation concerned itself so much with meditation, the metaphysics of consciousness, the
occult and psychic practices as they do
today. New York University, among other
well-known schools, offered courses in meditation, witchcraft, magic and Oriental religions. A strange "occult stew" of swamis,
sun-signs, gurus, mantras, witches, tarot
cards, yoga, and the I Ching has become the
current diet on many campuses. Meditation
in general, and Transcendental Meditation
(TM) in particular, became caught up in this
hodgepodge of sense and nonsense, making
it difficult for many people to appreciate the

17

essential value which meditation has to contribute to American life. It has begun to permeate the very air we breathe, leaving many uncertain whether to liken it to pollution that beclouds the senses, or to a fragrant incense.

With the rise of the Consciousness Revolution in the early Sixties, meditation, along with other altered states of consciousness, came to be looked upon as a form of secular religion. Sam Keen of the Behavioral Science Institute of California wrote that "this religion is eclectic, experimental, mystical and non-professional—a do-it-yourself kit composed of disciplines and insights drawn from many religions and occult traditions." (1)

The most popular technique, TM and its offshoot, Dr. Herbert Benson's Relaxation Response, * have nothing to do with religion, the occult or the drug culture. They *do* represent a major shift in American thinking. For some people, TM and the Relaxation Response are a turning away from traditional cultural values; for others, a re-discovery of those values. Knowledge is being sought not only through the logic, science and technology

* Since the TM technique and the Relaxation Response technique are similar, we will be using the term "TM technique" to designate both. See chapter Seven for the actual differences between the two.

to which the West, and America in particular, has always given primacy, but also from feeling, insight, inspiration, intuition, and from one of man's oldest means to knowledge —meditation. And although it is young people who have spear-headed this rebellion, men and women of all ages and from all walks of life have been increasingly drawn to meditation in their quest for self-improvement as well as new spiritual and cultural values.

To begin with, several books about meditation quickly made the bestseller lists. At local libraries across the country, meditation books of every type are continually in circulation. TM centers are enrolling thousands of students every week and are obviously enjoying tremendous growth. Popular television talk shows and magazines are highlighting and exploring the TM technique. Scholarly journals are reporting TM experiments and the scientific evidence that has been amassed to validate its many physiological claims. Within the churches, interest in meditation is increasing, and a new wave of layman participation is developing. Even people who are not directly involved in TM activities are curious and sometimes puzzled by them. Thus, this book is an attempt to teach those who are curious or puzzled about meditation and to assist them in making informed judgments as to what is believable and possible to achieve and what is not.

Where did this new interest in meditation come from?

Perhaps we are seeing a phenomenon produced, in part, by a space age; when people are more conscious of space, they become increasingly aware, as did the French mathematician Pascal, of their own significance. Landing on the moon may have had the salutary side-effect of making people more concerned with the meaning of their own lives. Is it really possible that a feat of technology could have precipitated a new interest in old beliefs? To a generation in school during the first moon walk, meditation has become a way of exploring "inner space" and re-establishing their own importance in the scheme of things.

The protest phenomenon has become yet another cause for the Consciousness Revolution. And although meditation may be a soft protest compared to others we have seen, it is a form of protest. In the words of Lewis Mumford, "the present revolt of the younger generation against the machine has made a practice of promoting disorder and randomness" (2) to replace our tightly controlled and instrumental society which we have lived with since the industrial revolution. The effects of meditation, like drugs, non-Western religions, spiritualism, and astrology, cannot be carefully programmed. It becomes a way to break out of the prescribed patterns of our ordered, rational and routine experience.

Our thinking about ourselves has been locked up in different materialistic dogmas for a long time, but now it appears that new findings in physics, biology, chemistry and other sciences are beginning to undermine materialism as a philosophy of life. On the basis of innumerable experiments with students of meditation, psychologists have reached the conclusion that the mind is capable of experiencing dimensions other than the one of our routine, daily life. The experience of meditation has taught hundreds of thousands of people that there is a sea of beauty, of life and love within each of us, and that we can contact this reality if we wish.

Why has the "TM technique" become the most popular form of meditation?

Because it has been most thoroughly researched and scientifically validated. Even though, on the one hand, we want to break out of the mechanized mold into which we have been cast, we are not altogether willing to forego the scientific proofs we have become so accustomed to having. Also, the "TM technique" is both easy and effective. It is ideally suited for the busy life of most Americans.

How does one learn to meditate "immediately?" Isn't there a contradiction there somewhere?

In a certain sense, yes. But not when one learns to appreciate the particular virtues of the "TM technique." We must all start from where we are at, and for most of us that means with a good deal of time pressure. It has almost become a national virtue to be in a rush. "A quiet moment for meditation" in our culture means just that—a moment. The student who once asked the Zen master, "I've got a few moments—can you teach me *satori*?" was serious—and that's the tragedy of it. *Satori*, or the moment of mystical illumination, may only be a moment, but it can not be learned in a moment. Learning to recognize the symphonics of our inner self is a long-time passion for the serious meditator. That means that most forms of meditation are out of reach for people in our clock-conscious culture. However, the "TM technique" being natural and easily taught, enables us to learn how to meditate quickly and easily, while at the same time teaching us the value of a slower-paced life.

Is there any other unique feature of the "TM technique" that makes it so popular?

There are several, but one which is especially relevant to our "Now . . . I want it NOW" culture. And that has to do with the problem of cultural noise. The movements of our mind are extremely subtle; to be in tune with them, one must find a quiet place and devote his entire attention to their detection. It is no accident that most meditators "contemplate from their own mountain peak." For many forms of meditation, the silent, uninterrupted life of the hermit is almost a prerequisite. In the United States, precious few mountain tops remain. Even if we assume the average person could detect the subtle awareness of his mind, how could he be expected to respond to it above the din and bustle of daily life? Nobody has ever heard a pin drop on the subway. A special value of the "TM technique," unlike other forms of meditation, is that it can be practiced anywhere, at any time . . . regardless of the decibel level.

But the "TM technique" is really just a fad, isn't it? Aren't people who practice TM really just playing a game with themselves?

Well, in any large movement, there are always going to be those who are insincere, perhaps without knowing it themselves, and those who find that meditation was not really what they were looking for at all. But certainly such is not true of the great mass of TM meditators who have found their lives enriched and have benefited from meditation in innumerable ways.

But this is a moment to be completely candid. (Candor about the TM movement, after all, was one of the purposes which brought this book into being.) There are undoubtedly people who feel the need today to play the new "heightened consciousness game" and perhaps it is these people who give meditation its undeserved "faddish image."

What meditation will be for you, however, depends upon how well you put into practice what you read in the following pages.

CHAPTER TWO

Can Meditation Be Learned From A Book?

Can Meditation be learned from a book?

Those who do not believe that a teacher is essential for serious meditation usually argue, "Well, if a teacher is necessary, who taught the first teacher?" They believe that only the externals, the technique of meditation can be taught, and that real enlightenment is provided by the experience of meditation itself. In a certain sense, they are right.

Meditation is a growth process. Many people confuse the techniques of meditation with the experience of meditation. The "TM technique" results in meditation, but while the technique itself remains unchanged from the first session, the continuing experience of meditation provides the meditator with ceaseless opportunities for inner change and

27

growth. In a very real sense, meditation is self-taught.

Although an instructor does provide an additional teaching dimension, virtually anything that can be taught, can be taught from a book. Indeed, far more difficult subject matters, such as foreign languages, calculus, law, can all be learned on one's own. Certainly, a teacher will make it much easier to learn, let us say, a foreign language, but you can learn a language without a teacher. The whole emphasis which TM people put upon personal instruction, as we shall see, is exaggerated; there is actually very little personal instruction in the TM course. Personal instruction is not essential; it is helpful. Obviously, where there is no teacher, for whatever reason, a "how to" book is a must.

Well, then, what should be the role of a teacher in meditation?

Because the experience of meditation is an intimate, personal one, the true "teacher," paradoxically, teaches by not teaching. He accepts each of his pupils for what they are and where they are on the path to self-awareness. He is like the parent who sets his child on the road of life and guides him a little way, but ultimately must lead him to find his own way

The best that a teacher can do is to indicate in the most general way the elements which are involved in meditation, and then let each man or woman find their own way by trial and error. No "Master" should be followed with blind trust; the only true master is your own "inner light." This point is beautifully made by Saint Theresa of Lisieux: "I know it seems easy to help souls, to make them love God above all and to mold them according to His will. But actually, without His help, it is easier to make the sun shine at night. One must banish one's own tastes and personal ideas and guide souls along the special way Jesus indicates for them rather than along one's own particular way." (3)

Why should I expect to learn how to practice the "TM technique" from this book? After all, I didn't learn how from the other books.
Most other books on the subject have assumed either that the "TM technique" can not be taught from a book or that the reader will eventually be taking the course. (These have been authored by TM proponents and/or teachers.) Here, we are assuming that, either for financial reasons, the unavailability of a TM center, or whatever, the reader will view this book as his only guide and that he will return to it from time to time, re-

freshing his mind on points he may have missed or forgotten.

For these reasons, far greater emphasis has been put upon the actual details and problems of learning to use the "TM technique." The questions have all been drawn from those asked during actual TM courses and the answers provided are, with few exceptions, the direct answers of instructors or are derived from TM lectures, and literature.

CHAPTER THREE

What Meditation Is—and Is Not

As a Westernized form of yoga, isn't the TM practice some kind of religion?

No, quite the opposite. It is probably *because* of their non-sectarian nature that such meditation methods as TM and the Relaxation Response have gained their current popularity. True, for many people these methods of meditation do give expression to their mystical and religious needs, but for most people these methods are popular because "they work."

Nevertheless, the TM method is still considered a religion by many people, including many churchmen. Part of the confusion arises because meditation was once a widespread practice among the laymen of the church, but eventually it fell into disuse. Now that meditation has arisen outside of

33

the church, many religious groups have attacked it. Perhaps they feel that meditation is a competitive path toward certain similar goals, i.e., inner peace, good will toward our neighbors, etc. . . . a path that can be traveled outside religion.

What is an "Altered State of Consciousness?" [ASC]
This is a general term which designates the research that is being done into sleep, dreams, trance, meditation, as well as other states of awareness. Meditation, like drugs or hypnosis, includes a wide variety of states of consciousness, depending upon the method of meditation adopted. In every case, however, an ASC is a departure from our day-to-day, waking consciousness, and may be either a transitory or permanent departure. They may be either "bad" (coma or drunkenness) or "good" (mystical enlightenment, meditation).

Isn't the objective of meditation similar to that of self-hypnosis?
Absolutely not. Meditation is very different from trance, hypnosis, and other altered states of consciousness, since the meditator does not seek to lose consciousness but, on the contrary, seeks to expand it. Nor is meditation to be confused with pray-

er. Perhaps this is a good time to make clear what meditation *is not*. In this connection, James Martineau, a nineteenth-century British theologian, has given us this very clear and helpful statement: "There is an act of the mind, natural to the earnest and the wise, impossible only to the sensual and the fool, healthful to all who are sincere, which has small place in modern usage and which few can distinguish from vacuity. Those who knew what it was called it *meditation*. It is not Reading, in which we apprehend the thoughts of others. It is not Study, in which we strive to master the known and prevail over it till it lies in order beneath our feet. It is not Deliberation, which reckons up the forces which surround our individual lot and projects accordingly the expedient on the right. It is not Self-scrutiny, which by itself is only shrewdness. Its view is not personal and particular, but universal and immense. It brings not an intense self-consciousness and spiritual egotism, but almost a renunciation of individuality. It gives us no matter for criticism and doubt, but everything for wonder and love . . .

"Let any man go into the Silence; strip himself of all pretence and selfishness and sensuality and sluggishness of soul; lift off thought after thought, passion after passion till he reaches the inmost depths of all, and it will be strange if he does not feel the Eternal Presence close upon his soul . . ."

How do we scientifically determine the differences between meditation and other states of consciousness?

The primary instrument is the electroencephalograph (EEG), which measures and records the fluctuations in the brain-wave patterns which our brains are constantly emitting.

What exactly are brain-wave patterns?

For convenience, the usual brain-wave patterns during sleep and waking are classified according to the amount of voltage in the electrical charges (amplitude) and the speed of change (frequency). The four known brain waves include the Beta wave (13 to 30 cycles-per-second), which is associated with mental concentration, visual tracing, and problem solving; Alpha (8 to 12 cycles-per-second), signifying states of relaxed alertness and defocused attention—floating, peaceful meditation; Theta (4 to 7 cycles-per-second), which is linked to reverie and creativity—half conscious awareness of subconscious imagery; and Delta (.05 to 3 cycles-per-second), occurring during sleep, usually dreamless sleep.

How can one prove that the mental state induced by the "TM technique" really differs from that of hypnosis?

In hypnotic trance, the Alpha rhythms remain the same as those in our normal, waking state. There is also no change in our metabolism, such as occurs in meditation. The physiological patterns during hypnosis have no relation to those we have noticed during meditation. During hypnosis visceral changes and brain-wave patterns take the form characteristic of the mental state that has been suggested to the subject. The belief therefore that hypnosis is "the poor man's meditation—Western meditation" is an erroneous one.

The "deep rest" during the TM session is really just like sleep, isn't it?

There are certain similarities, but although sleep also involves the dissolution of ego boundaries and the altering of our consciousness, as does hypnosis to a presumably lesser extent, and despite other superficial similarities between sleep and meditation, there remain wide differences. With regard to sleep, a primary difference is that the meditator remains, except in the most extreme instances, aware of his surroundings to a far greater extent than a sleeping person, even though he may not respond to changes going on around him. During sleep, the consumption of oxygen decreases and carbon dioxide in the blood increases appreciably only after several hours, whereas in meditation such changes occur quickly. These signs, as well as an increase in blood acidity are due to a decrease in ventilation and not to a change in metabolism such as occurs during meditation. The rate and amount of skin resistance is much less in sleep than in meditation, and EEG patterns are significantly different.

What is the basic difference between meditation and other states of altered consciousness?

Upon the physiological evidence now available, it appears that the withdrawal of consciousness from the world around us takes one of two basic forms: one which increases the excitation of the mind, and the other which increases its tranquility. The former includes the creative, psychotic, and other hallucinatory states; the latter comprises progressively intense degrees of meditation, from simple contemplation, such as musing over a passage in the Holy Bible, through Zen to Yoga *samadhi*. In other words, virtually every other form of altered consciousness, *except meditation*, will make the mind and body hyper-active; meditation relaxes both mind and body.

What makes meditation different from trance?

Trance, whether spontaneous or brought about by a hypnotist, is in many ways an extension of the day-dreaming state in which a person's awareness is focused and directed inward rather than outward. Apart from the physiological differences between trance and meditation, which we have already mentioned, meditation also differs from trance psychologically. All meditation is purposeful in its nature; trance is not. The "TM technique" differs even further in that it is unfocused, expanded awareness; trance is a highly focused state of awareness.

What is the difference between meditation and contemplation?

"Meditation" is one of those words defined more by the way we use it than by any denotive meaning. We all know, more or less, what is meant when someone uses it. We know that the person is referring to a state of reverie, of musing or reflecting, of careful consideration, of conceiving a plan or design, or of religious devotion or discipline. It is also often used in such a way as to become confused with similar but distinctly different states such as trance, ecstasy, and the "creative moment."

Meditation, as it is understood by the TM method, is quite different from contemplation. Contemplation is actively *thinking about* something (a physical object, a passage from a book, a philosophical idea). Because of its highly conscious nature, contemplation is more closely akin to problem solving than to meditation.

Still another difference is pointed out by Harold Bloomfield, *et. al*; during contemplation ". . . the thought will sustain its expansive effect only as long as a person continues to think about it . . . What is constant in a person's experience is not the object of experience but the conscious experiencer. If a person wishes to make lasting changes in his experience, what he needs is not a change in what he is thinking *about* but in what he is thinking *with*. To achieve this change he must use a technique which expands the range of consciousness itself." (4) Meditation provides just such a technique, and because it does, it differs from contemplation.

What is the difference between meditation and concentration?

In terms of the psychology of meditation, there seem to be two general types of meditation. The first, a concentrative meditation, which involves a restriction of awareness, focusing the attention on an object or bodily function (such as breathing) or the rigid repetition of a word (mantra) or movement (mudra). The second, a nonfocused, nonconcentrative meditation which is designed to "open up" awareness. The TM method belongs to this last group.

CHAPTER FOUR

The Mantra Question

What is a mantra?

"Mantra" is a Sanskrit word which designates "a thought-sound the effects of which are known." The "meaning" of a mantra consists of its vibratory effect on different portions of the brain, such as would be felt if it were being said aloud.

The mantra is used in TM meditation initially to focus the field of attention.

Why is a mantra important to meditation?

A mantra, as such, is not important to meditation, but it is essential to the TM technique as taught by Maharishi Mahesh Yogi. However, nearly every form of meditation requires some mental device equivalent to the mantra. In terms of the psychology of awareness, the important thing about a mantra is that it is the "ticket" to expanded awareness.

Which other forms of meditation use mantras?

A well-known yoga practice you may have actually seen involves the use of the Hare Krishna mantra which is always chanted aloud in a group. Among Zen masters, a common mantra is "Mu," a sound which has no meaning in Japanese. Among the Dervish sect of the Sufis, "Ya Haadi!" (O Guide!) is repeated faster and faster as they match their dance movements to the repetitions. Prayer practices in the Christian Church have similarities and perhaps even have their origins in the mantric form of meditation. St. John Climacus wrote: "If many words are used in prayer, all sorts of distracting pictures hover in the mind but worship is lost. If little is said or only a single word is said, the mind remains concentrated." In the Judaic tradition, the secret names for Yaweh (God) were often intoned, and thus served as mantras.

These are just a few examples to underscore the fact that mantras are nothing new and are certainly not unique to TM.

Doesn't the use of the mantra involve a lot of concentration?

No. The "TM technique" is not a concentrative form of meditation; it is designed to "open up" the awareness. The meditator is not supposed to dwell on the mantra or in any way seek to control its use, such as timing its silent repetition with his breathing or any physical movements.

The meditator is encouraged to let his attention flow naturally, expending no mental energy through concentration. The experience of pure awareness is thus achieved through a "letting go," the unwilled quieting of the mind so that it settles down quite naturally into its own inner nature.

CHAPTER FIVE

Selecting a Mantra

How do TM instructors select personal mantras?

Many mistakenly believe that no two people in the world have the same mantra. Such is not the case. (The author knows of one student who became intensely discouraged when he found two other students who had "his" mantra.) Such an attitude is quite wrong. When you are given a "personal mantra," you are given a mantra which is presumably "right" for you. That does not mean that it may not also be "right" for someone else.

There is also the experience of one skeptical student who enrolled at three different TM centers and received the same mantra all three times. How do we account for this experience? Are the instructors psychic? They disclaim any such ability. Can they be so well trained in the few weeks they learn mantra selection? Most gurus study with their disciples for years before they acquire such insight. Where then may the answer lie?

Ostensibly, the instructor goes into "meditation" and by this means is able to give the student his mantra. Such may indeed be the case, but it seems at least as likely that the selection of the mantra is made through some largely mechanical means. Most likely it is determined by factors such as one's name, occupation, age, marital status, or a combination of these . . . data which are requested on the questionnaire the student filled out prior to meeting the teacher.

It is also not unlikely that the selection of a mantra may be arrived at through numerology, as we will teach the reader to do in this chapter. If nothing else, this method has the virtue of being no more mechanical than the technique most likely employed by the teachers of TM.

Why is the selection of a personal mantra so important?

There are a great many authorities who say that it isn't. They stress the universality of meditation techniques and believe that the primary effect of meditation can be evoked by any process of repetition. Their belief, however, need not necessarily conflict with the contention of the Maharishi Mahesh Yogi, the founder of the TM movement, that a mantra may have an additional specific effect on specific people.

Under ideal conditions, the guru bestows a mantra upon his disciple, (of whom he has personal knowledge) only after years of training in more and more advanced meditation. Clearly, such can not be the case with the TM course, nor is it possible for us to do so in this book. What is possible is to enable the reader to find his own mantra by a means no more mechanical than those probably used in an actual TM course.

What is important is that the student does not select his own mantra because he "likes it," but that it in some sense be given to him. (The fact that he "likes it," could interfere with his meditation.) The method devised in this book prevents any arbitrary emotional selection and, at the same time, provides the reader with a mantra on a highly personal basis.

How can I acquire my own personal mantra without enrolling in a TM class?

Your name and birth date are two of the most personal things about you. Therefore, let us use them as the basic determinants for your individual Sanskrit mantra.

On the following pages you will find a simple system of numerical calculations which were used in ancient times to determine the vibrations existing between letters and certain numbers. This system is based on the Hebraic Kabbala which was chosen because it is much less complicated than other numerical techniques.

The 26 letters of the alphabet correspond to the 9 single digit numbers. Consequently, more than one letter corresponds to the same number, as shown below:

1	2	3	4	5	6	7	8	9
A	B	C	D	E	F	G	H	I
J	K	L	M	N	O	P	Q	R
S	T	U	V	W	X	Y	Z	

Letters A, J and S have the same numerical value: 1. The letters B, K, and T have the value of 2, and so forth. The ancients believed that whatever number a letter is under, this is its numerical power or number vibration in the Heavenly Spheres.

Since most names will translate into two digits, let us use the name Samuel Jones as our first example:

S - 1	J - 1
A - 1	O - 6
M - 4	N - 5
U - 3	E - 5
E - 5	S - 1
L - 3	18
17	

The name Samuel corresponds to the number 17 and the name Jones to the number 18. To secure the full name vibration, it is necessary to add 17 and 18, which gives us 35. This is a double number, so we multiply its components, 3 and 5, to get 15. This is the Name Number of this particular person.

In rare instances when the Name Number is a single digit, we would multiply that number times itself. For example, with the name Al Bas:

A - 1	B - 2
L - 3	A - 1
4	S - 1
	4

Following the same procedure as above, we would add 4 and 4, which gives us the single digit of eight. Since there are not two digits to be multiplied, as there were with 3 and 5, we would simply multiply 8 times itself, yielding 64. This would then be the Name Number of this particular person.

We will now suppose that the birth-date of our original example, Samuel Jones, is January 1, 1949. Because January is the first month of the year, it translates into the number 1. (If it were February, it would translate into 2, March into 3, and so forth.) The numbers in the birthdate remain as they are. When we add these numbers, we get a total of 25.

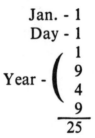

$$
\begin{array}{rl}
\text{Jan. -} & 1 \\
\text{Day -} & 1 \\
\text{Year -} & \left(\begin{array}{l} 1 \\ 9 \\ 4 \\ 9 \end{array}\right. \\
\hline
& 25
\end{array}
$$

This total of 25 is a double number, so we multiply 2 and 5, which equals 10. Samuel Jones' Birth Number is 10.

The Name Number of Samuel Jones (15) indicates the first half of his mantra (lah), the fifteenth phoenetic sound of the Sanskrit alphabet (see page 59). His Birth Number (10) indicates the second half of his mantra (hah), or the tenth phoenetic sound of the Sanskrit alphabet. Therefore, the mantra of Samuel Jones would be "Lah hah," pronounced as a single word, with no

56

break between the syllables.

Should the Name Number or the Birth Number contain double digits whose product is greater than 27 (the number of different phoenetic sounds in the Sanskrit alphabet), then merely subtract 27 from the product. For example, should the components of the Name Number be 4 and 7, whose product is 28, we would subtract 27 from 28, which gives us 1. (The first half of the mantra would then be the first phoenetic sound of the Sanskrit alphabet.) If the Name Number or the Birth Number still exceeds 27, repeat the process and again subtract 27 from the number. For example, let us suppose the Name or Birth Number were 81. We would subtract 27, yielding 54. Repeating the process, we would again subtract 27 from 54, yielding 27.

Should a double digit number end in zero (10, 20, 30, 40, etc.), drop the zero and the remaining number designates the phoenetic sound in the Sanskrit alphabet. This sound becomes the first half of your mantra if derived from your Name Number, or the second half if derived from your Birth Number.

If you do not wish a Sanskrit mantra, you might heed the suggestion of Dr. Herbert Benson and simply select a word or sound, such as "one," "love," "peace," or even the time-honored "Om." A possible difficulty with choosing your own mantra is that you are too apt to choose a word whose meaning you like, or a sound which is particularly pleasant to you. While this initially may be helpful to you, making it easier to retain the mantra in your thoughts, ultimately it may be more difficult to reach a state of "pure awareness," wherein even the mantra is no longer held in one's thoughts. For this reason, we suggest the standard TM practice of using a Sanskrit mantra which will be meaningless to you. If nothing else, the procedure outlined above should produce a totally meaningless mantra sound.

MANTRA PRONUNCIATION

One of the most common of the Indic alphabets is the nagari script. In Sanskrit, the individual letters as a rule express not only a vowel or only a consonant but a consonant with a vowel following. The vowel which follows is usually *a*. We have adopted this procedure below, so that consonants are to be pronounced with a broad *a* (or "ah") sound following them.

Birth or name number	Sanskrit letter	Phoenetic sound
1	अ	uh (as in "the")
2	आ	ah
3	ऐ	i (as in "eye")
4	औ	ow (as in "how")
5	ब्	bah
6	छ्	chah
7	ड्	dah
8	ए	ay (as in "way")
9	ग्	gah
10	ह्	hah
11	इ	ih (as in "in")
12	ई	ee (as in "we")
13	ज्	jah (as in "jolly")
14	क्	kah
15	ल्	lah
16	म	mah
17	न	nah
18	ओ	oh
19	प	pah

Birth or name number	Sanskrit letter	Phoenetic sound
20	र्	rah
21	स्	sah
22	ष्	shah
23	त्	tah
24	थ्	thah
25	ऊ	ooh (as in "ooze")
26	व्	vah
27	य्	yah (as in "yacht")

CHAPTER SIX

How to Master the "TM Technique"
Plus Questions and Answers

A. THE TM PROGRAM

Let us begin by describing the overall program one would face upon enrolling in a TM course.

The program begins with two introductory lectures, both free to the public. In the first lecture, the physical and mental benefits of the TM technique are described and the instructor reviews the validation research which has taken place. The second, or preparatory lecture, covers the mechanics of the technique itself and prepares a person to learn it. How the TM technique differs from other forms of meditation as well as the background from which it derives are also discussed.

There are three basic requirements for

enrolling in the TM program. The first is that the program be completed on four successive days, and new members are allowed to begin only when they can attend four days in a row. The second requirement, of course, is a fee. For the fee one receives the initial instruction, a lifetime membership in the International Meditation Society (IMS), an optional once-a-month check on your meditation practices to ensure they are being performed properly, and a continuing series of advanced lectures. The fees themselves, as of this writing, are $55.00 (for high school students), $65.00 (for college students), $125.00 (for adults), and $200.00 (for married couples, including children under age sixteen).

The third requirement is to abstain from the use of all "recreational drugs" for at least fifteen days before beginning. By "recreational drugs," the TM people mean all drugs not prescribed by a physician. The effects of these drugs remain within the body, altering the functioning of the central nervous system thereby preventing the effectiveness of TM practice.

On the first day, during the "hour" of personal instruction, the student is asked to bring some fresh flowers, fresh fruits and a new white handkerchief. These the teacher uses in a ceremony during which he expresses his gratitude for the TM teaching and prepares himself to hand it down to the student. This ceremony is not a religious one and the student is not asked to participate but only to bear witness.

During this session, the student is given his personal mantra and is instructed in how to use it. He is then left alone to meditate while the teacher passes on to the next student.

At the group meetings on the following days, there are usually many questions from the new meditators. The teacher answers them and makes suggestions. At the second group meeting, the teacher explains the possible experiences that occur during meditation and how they may be best understood and handled. At the third group meeting, the teacher reviews practical hints on meditating, emphasizes the importance of experience in understanding meditation, and tells the student meditator about the advanced courses which are open to him.

All of the important points included in the actual TM program are covered in this book—with two obvious exceptions: there is no one-to-one personal instruction nor does a TM teacher bestow a personal mantra upon the reader. However, this book serves as your teacher and you should already have your mantra from the preceding chapter.

B. HOW TO MEDITATE

When and how often to meditate.

That will depend upon your individual schedule; everyone's lifestyle is different. The recommended times, however, are suited to the lives most people lead. If possible, the first session should be in the morning before breakfast. At this time, the meditator prepares himself for the eight hours of activity which are to follow. After the day is over, and before the evening meal, another session should be held. This session prepares the meditator for the evening ahead.

Length of the meditation session.

Twenty minutes is the time recommended by the Maharishi and his instructors. But usually this period is preceded and concluded by a three minute "going-in" and "coming-out" transition period.

Where to meditate.

With a little practice, one can learn to meditate anywhere, even on a crowded subway or bus. Ideally, however, any quiet place will do, any place where one is relatively free from distractions and sudden interruptions. Choose a place where the light is dim and that is reasonably free from noise. However, regardless of how noisy it may be, as long as you can think, you can meditate.

The need for special clothing.

You can wear special clothing if you want to, but there is not much point in it. It won't make a bit of difference . . . assuming your clothing is not uncomfortable.

Posture and relaxing the body.

Once, when the author had just begun to meditate, and long before the "TM technique" was known to him, he joined a well-meaning and diligent meditation group and was given a mimeographed sheet with explicit and lengthy instructions on *How to Relax the Physical Body*. However sincerely meant, and despite the fact that it seemed to work for some, the author spent some of his time trying to remember if he had remembered everything, and became as nervous as a cat walking on a balloon. "How loose should I get? Am I too loose? How can I be loose with a straight spine? Why must both feet be on the floor and the hands not touching? (The Buddha's favorite position violates both.) What happens if some of the air slips into my lungs instead of my diaphragm?"

This was the author's first experience at meditation, but fortunately he did not give it up; he simply gave up that particular group of meditators.

The best place to meditate is on a chair or couch; don't lie down on a couch. Sit up straight, but no more rigidly than may be required to hold your shoulders back. Keep the spinal column free of those twists and turns which normally bad posture may give you. Do not try to do more than that.

Fold your hands if you wish, let them lie in your lap or at your sides, or anywhere else that makes you feel comfortable. Basically, just try to forget about them. As for your feet, most people keep them flat on the floor without thinking about it. That is the important thing, not thinking about it. But you can assume the Lotus position if you wish . . . and if you are comfortable doing it.

Breathing through the nose is always preferable to breathing through the mouth, and one should become accustomed to keeping one's mouth closed during meditation.

Preparing the mind for meditation—"going-in."

For the first few seconds or minute, let your eyes stay open and gaze at some convenient object. One of your hands will do—but don't think about it, just see it. (And don't think about "just seeing it" either.) Then let your eyes close and relax without attempting to say your mantra. Having "gazed" prior to closing your eyes, your mind will be relatively free of thoughts, but being aware of the feeling of your body relaxing can be a further help.

Thinking the mantra.(See Chapter Five before continuing)

Each meditation begins by thinking the mantra. It will probably come to your mind naturally after you have been consciously relaxed yourself. If not, begin thinking it to yourself and, *if you can*, remain with it throughout your meditation. It will naturally take you to the awareness levels you are attempting to reach. However, *if you become aware* that you are no longer thinking the mantra, come back to it again. In other words, whenever you have the choice of what to think, choose the mantra.

Completing the meditation—"coming-out."

The final three minutes, "swimming back to the surface," as it were, is largely just the reverse of the initial three minutes. Keep your eyes closed and let your mind "wander" over your body. You will feel your muscle tone gradually restoring itself, your senses becoming "alive" again. Slowly open your eyes. Do not rush this transition; you will find that it varies somewhat from session to session.

C. AM I DOING IT CORRECTLY?
Questions and Answers

How will I know when the twenty minutes are up? Should I set an alarm clock for the right intervals?

Absolutely not. Simply arrange a clock so that you can see it easily by opening your eyes and without having to move excessively. Most importantly, do not worry about the time. Initially, you will find that far less time has elapsed than you thought. Later, you will find that the time has passed far more quickly than you thought. As your experience of meditation matures, you will find that you are able to judge time passing without any problem—and without any consciousness of it.

What happens if I get drowsy and let my mouth fall open or my head nod down?

If you do not become aware of it, you will do nothing about it. If you do become aware of it, don't panic, don't feel you've done anything "wrong." Just resume your initial position and continue meditating.

What do I do if the phone rings?

If you are expecting an important call, delay your meditation. Otherwise, take the phone off the hook. Advise your friends of what you are doing at these particular half hours in the day and ask them not to call you at those times. They will respect what you are doing.

What if the doorbell rings?

This noise will, of course, register on your consciousness, but as you become more experienced in meditation, it will not disturb you. You will have a flicker of detached awareness. But unless you sense it is an emergency, do not answer it. Anything that was important enough to bring a neighbor to your door, if it was really important, will bring him back.

Should I time the thinking of my mantra with my breathing?

Absolutely not. But don't worry about it, because you are probably going to do it anyway. Initially, nothing is more natural than to time one's mantra with one's breath. Possibly you will find each session begins in this manner. Let it. We normally breathe at about the rate of sixteen breaths per minute, or slightly less. As we begin to sink into meditation, the rate of our breathing decreases. Even if we instinctively "time" our mantras to our breathing, the two will soon become desynchronized.

71

What happens if my awareness strays away from saying the mantra?

It will. Don't let that worry you. Eventually the mantra will be replaced by stray thoughts that will come into your mind. These are thoughts that have to surface to be "worked-out." Remember, when you have the choice, simply return to thinking the mantra.

What happens if I begin to mispronounce my mantra?

Nothing. This is known as "losing" one's mantra. It happens quite often. You may find yourself saying, for example, "Sha-*heh*" instead of "Shee-*hah*." You may deal with this problem in the same way you deal with random thoughts. If you become aware that you are mispronouncing your mantra, simply choose the correct pronunciation.

Does practicing aloud help?

No. If you do you will develop a "mental voice," and you will begin to *hear* the mantra as if you were reciting passages of poetry to yourself. The mantra should be thought, not heard. The sound of your own voice in your mind becomes a distraction. You will understand this problem better when we discuss meditation in general, rather than merely the "TM technique."

How will I know if I am "coming-out" of meditation too quickly?

You will know. Just as you cannot *will* yourself into meditation with the "TM technique," so you cannot return too quickly from a session without knowing it. Your mind and body will now be experiencing a state of deep rest and quiet. With any abrupt return, your nervous system will experience a "shock" of discomfort. The feeling will not be unlike "having to get up in the morning." (You may even suffer a headache.) Therefore, be sure to take the full three minutes to "come-out."

How should I feel after meditating?

You will probably feel as if you have just awakened from an afternoon nap, except that your relaxation was much deeper, and with that will come an unusual amount of energy and an intense awareness of everything around you.

What am I doing wrong if I keep getting aches and pains in different parts of my body as a result of meditating?

Many of these aches and pains are caused by the release of tensions. (Assuming you are not "coming-out" too quickly.) We all have "tension points" in our bodies which react quickly to our *becoming* tense. With many people, these stress areas react also with the *release* of tensions.

Why should I not meditate after meals?
        If you have just eaten, your body is sending an increased amount of blood to the abdomen. As a result, less blood, and therefore less oxygen, is flowing through your brain. You will feel that "after-dinner" sleepiness. Therefore, wait at least one hour after eating before you attempt to meditate . . . assuming you're not able to meditate prior to your first and last meals of the day.

Why should I not meditate before retiring for the night?
        If you do, you will most likely find yourself bursting with energy and wide awake. If you continue meditating before bedtime, you may turn yourself into a chronic insomniac.

Aren't there dangerous side-effects to practicing the "TM technique?"
        If you practice the technique according to the instructions given, it is a harmless and pleasant experience.
        However, the "TM technique" is not

a parlor game. It is a potentially powerful instrument of the mind and *in* the mind. If it were not, the "TM technique" could not produce the many benefits which it does. For that reason, it should never be misused or used carelessly.

However, individuals with a history of mental illness may undergo severe relapses if they practice *any* form of meditation without responsible supervision. Although the "TM technique" is used successfully to help mentally disturbed people, it must be remembered that the technique, in such cases, is also being practiced under the direction of a physician.

Dr. Leon S. Otis, director of the Psycho-Biology and Physiology Department of Stanford Research Institute, warns: "People with histories of serious psychological or psychosomatic problems have been known to suffer recurrences when they start meditating. The mind is not a blank during TM—thoughts tend to float. Some people freak out!" (5)

However, the "TM technique" practiced by people with "normal" mental and physical health, and practiced as prescribed, does not present any dangers.

If I have an argument with my mate, or the kids get into trouble, or a business deal falls

through, will it do me any good to sit down and meditate?

Well, it won't do you any harm, but it probably won't do you much good either. The benefits of the "TM technique" are long-ranged; it is not like popping a tranquilizer. The "TM technique" will enable you to deal more effectively with all types of crisis situations because you will not be as tense. Some people respond more quickly to a brief period of meditation, but there is a danger in that, too. Meditation is not like "counting to ten" when you are upset; it is far more effective. So it should never be used in such a way that it becomes a crutch.

Does it take a great deal of willpower or self-control to master the "TM technique"?

Not a great deal, but it does take *some*. The "TM technique" itself is effortless—if it is practiced properly. But you must give twenty minutes each morning and evening to the technique. It is not essential that it be morning and evening, if your particular schedule makes that difficult, but it is important that the times you choose be regular ones. Regularity in meditation has a deciding power over your success. Without it nothing can be done, because "occasional" attempts to practice the "TM technique" are largely a waste of time. Therefore, the exact hour should be chosen, which is the most suitable and disturbance free, and unless something very unusual comes up, it should be adhered to.

While this may seem to require will-power, you will find that very quickly it becomes a habit—and habits require no will-power.

If two, daily sessions of meditation will benefit me, why won't it help me to meditate more often or for a longer period than 20 minutes?

Because the benefits of meditating do not derive merely from meditation itself. To secure the full benefits from meditation, a student must retain the balance between rest and activity. One can loose this balance by meditating too much. The feeling which will result from over-meditating is not unlike that which comes from oversleeping. One feels mildly groggy throughout most of the day. For this reason, it is suggested that the student only meditate twice a day, once in the morning and once in the early evening for approximately 20 minutes per session.

CHAPTER SEVEN

TM and the Relaxation Response
Similarities and Differences

What is the "fight-or-flight" response?

We all have this innate physiological reaction in us, and it is triggered whenever we are faced with stressful situations. It is the involuntary, physical responses which we have to situations which require us to make adjustments in our behavior, including increased blood pressure, heart rate, rate of breathing, muscle blood flow, and metabolism. These are all signs that we are making up our minds to handle the situation either through conflict or by escaping it.

What is the Relaxation Response?

If we have a continual need to adjust to stressful events which bring about the fight-or-flight response with all of its harmful bodily changes, it is natural to ask if nature did not also provide us with an inborn response which counteracts the effects of the fight-or-flight response. Such was the question which prompted the research of cardiologist Herbert Benson. He found that there is such a response which our bodies make and describes it in his own words: "Each of us possess a natural and innate protective mechanism against 'overstress,' which allows us to turn off harmful bodily effects, to counter the effects of the fight-or-flight response. This response against 'overstress' brings on bodily changes that decrease heart rate, lower metabolism, decrease the rate of breathing, and bring the body back into what is probably a healthier balance. This is the Relaxation Response." (6)

Does city living go hand in hand with the development of the fight-or-flight response?
Unquestionably. The primary cause of stress and hypertension is other people, particularly in large quantities. The way of life demanded by urban living contributes innumerable secondary causes, such as fear of losing one's job, taxes, mortgages, increased arguments with one's spouse, violations of the law, moving to a new home. There are as well innumerable, but unavoidable stresses to which we are subject merely by being alive: marriage, pregnancies and

birth, death of a loved one, changes in our health, a son or daughter leaving home, etc. Even where to go on our vacation and Christmas can be times of tension. Not to mention tension caused by the news media and popular "fright films" such as *Jaws, The Exorcist,* etc.

However, the basic cause of tension and stress for most people is the social environment which big-city living brings. But since we are not willing to forego the values which our civilization offers, and which depend so much on urban life, we must learn to live with the disadvantages as well as the advantages.

What are the essential elements of the Relaxation Response?

According to its discoverer, Dr. Herbert Benson, there are four essentials: (1) a mental device, (2) a quiet place, (3) a comfortable position for the body, and (4) a passive attitude.

The mental device may be either a mantra or other word, phrase, or sound said silently or aloud . . . or even an object to gaze at. If your eyes are closed, you may use either a word or sound mantra; if they are kept open, it is better to use an object mantra. Dr. Benson advises also that if you use rhythmic breathing, it should be timed to the repetition of the "mantra."

Choosing quietude means a place with as few distractions as possible. The quiet aids the repetition of the mantra in producing the needed calm. One may choose to meditate outdoors.

You should choose a position which you feel you can maintain for twenty minutes without muscular tension. While some people choose the cross-legged "lotus" position, most prefer simply to sit. Various postures such as kneeling, swaying, squatting prevent the meditator from falling asleep. Do not lie down because, in that position, the Relaxation Response will lead to sleep.

While you are thus completely relaxed physically, let your mind become aware of your breathing. Breathe through your nose, easily and naturally. Each time you breathe out, say the word "one" silently to yourself (or use another mental device as previously mentioned).

Continue in this manner for twenty minutes. You may open your eyes from time to time to check the clock, but as with the TM technique do not use an alarm. When you finish, sit quietly for a few minutes, at first with your eyes closed and later with them open.

In conclusion, Dr. Benson gives the following words of advice, which differ little from what we have been saying with regard to the TM technique: "Don't worry about whether you are successful in achieving a deep level of relaxation. Maintain a passive attitude and permit relaxation to occur at its own pace. When distracting thoughts occur, try to ignore them by not dwelling upon them and return to repeating 'ONE.' With practice the response should come with little effort. Practice the technique once or twice daily, but not within two hours after any meal, since the digestive processes seem to interfere with the elicitation of the Relaxation Response." (7)

Can hypnosis achieve the same effect as the Relaxation Response?

If the suggestion of deep rest is implanted in the subject, yes. Following the standard induction methods of hypnosis (or auto-suggestion for self-hypnosis), the subjects are relaxed with their eyes closed, while the suggestion to relax is repeated. Hypnosis itself does not produce any distinct physiological changes, but produces changes typical of the suggested state, and thus the Relaxation Response may be brought about.

What are the basic differences between the TM method and the Relaxation Response?

The differences are few but extremely

significant. First, the use of a mantra. Dr. Benson himself has commented on this key difference: ". . . we believe it is not necessary to use the specific method and specific *secret* sound taught by Transcendental Meditation. *Tests at the Thorndike Memorial Laboratory of Harvard have shown that a similar technique used with any sound or phrase or prayer or mantra brings forth the same physiologic changes noted during Transcendental Meditation . . ."* (8)

There is a further difference in that there is no insistence on the part of Dr. Benson that the Relaxation Response be learned through personal instruction. Indeed, there is nowhere one could go to learn it; Dr. Benson himself is concerned with experimenting, not with teaching.

CHAPTER EIGHT

The Physical Benefits of Meditation

What are the physical benefits of meditation?

Research indicates that meditators exhibit the physical signs of what has been described as a "wakeful, hypometabolic" state: reductions in oxygen consumption, carbon dioxide elimination and the rate and volume of respiration; a slight increase in the acidity of the arterial blood; a marked decrease in the blood-lactate level; a slowing of the heartbeat; a considerable increase in skin resistance, and an electroencephalogram pattern of the brain waves which show an intensification of alpha waves with an occasional theta-wave activity. Sounds like quite a lot, doesn't it? Well, it is. So let us review each of these effects and explain and examine them more thoroughly.

What has the metabolic rate got to do with "levels of rest?"

A decrease in oxygen consumption and the metabolic rate are indicators of the "level of rest" which has been achieved.

R.K. Wallace and Herbert Benson undertook their own experiments with 20 and 15 student subjects respectively. After their Harvard subjects were invited to meditate with the TM method, both the rate of oxygen consumption and carbon dioxide elimination decreased markedly. (Consumption and elimination returned to the pre-meditation level soon after the subjects stopped meditating.) During meditation, oxygen consumption fell from 251 cubic centimeters per minute to 211 cubic centimeters. Similarly, carbon dioxide elimination decreased from 219 centimeters per minute to 187 cubic centimeters. The conclusion which Wallace and Benson drew from their experiment was the "ratio of carbon dioxide elimination to oxygen consumption (in volume) remained essentially unchanged throughout . . . which indicates that the controlling factor for both was the rate of metabolism." (9)

Will I be able to control my heart rate through TM meditation?

Practicing the "TM technique" results in stabilizing the entire voluntary nervous system, so that the heart rate is slowed automatically. However, the "TM technique" is not intended to teach one to "control" any specific bodily function.

Thomas Routt studied twelve meditators, with a mean experience of thirteen months practicing the "TM technique," and compared them with a control group of non-meditators. He found notable differences in the two groups' heart rates before, during, and after meditation. The heart rates of the meditators were slower by ten to eleven beats per minute. (10) (11)

Is the "TM technique" effective in reducing high blood pressure?

The measurement of arterial blood pressure in meditating subjects has been found by Dr. Neal Miller and others to fall to "a rather low level," simply by "thinking it down." (12) The degree of control exhibited in these and other experiments has indicated two things: (1) that the rate of blood flow is controlled basically by constriction of the blood vessels, and (2) that persons suffering from hypertension or migraines can "learn" relief through meditation using the "TM technique."

Dr. Herbert Benson comments as follows: "While the fight-or-flight response is associated with the overactivity of the sympathetic nervous system, there is another response which leads to a quieting of the same nervous system. Indeed, there is evidence that hypertensive subjects can lower their blood pressure by regularly eliciting this other response. This is the Relaxation Response, an opposite, involuntary response that causes a reduction in the activity of the sympathetic nervous system . . . (13) (14) (15).

What is the significance of the GSR, and what has it got to do with meditation?

The GSR (Galvanic Skin Response) measures the resistance of the skin to an electrical current. This measure is thought by some to reflect the level of anxiety. A decrease in skin resistance represents a greater anxiety; a rise in resistance, greater relaxation. During the meditation of student subjects practicing the TM method, R.K. Wallace and Herbert Benson noted (16) that their skin resistance to an electrical current increased markedly, in some cases more than fourfold.

What are lactates, and what have they to do with anxiety?

Lactates are the waste products which our metabolism sends into the body. Measurements of the lactate level in the blood (another measurement of the body's "alarm system") have shown it to decline rapidly during meditation. Patients with an anxiety neurosis show a large rise in blood lactate when they are placed under stress (17), and an infusion of lactate has been shown to bring on anxiety attacks in normal subjects. But during meditation with the "TM technique," the lactate level fell nearly four times faster than the rate for people in a resting position or in the subjects themselves during their premeditation period of relaxation. (18)

We have mentioned the breath a lot in connection with the "TM technique." Is my breathing also another sign of relaxation?

Definitely. Just as one of the signs of the fight-or-flight response is a quickening of our breathing, so a slowing down of our respiratory system is one of the signs of relaxation. We normally breathe at the rate of about 16 breaths per minute, but during meditation with the "TM technique," we draw only about 8 to 10 breaths per minute and our breathing becomes more shallow.

The ratio of carbon dioxide elimination to oxygen consumption (in volume) remains essentially unchanged before, during, and after meditation. This indicates that the controlling factor for both was the metabolic rate. The reduction in the need for oxygen while meditating with the "TM technique" was reflected in the involuntary decrease in the rate of respiration and in the volume of air breathed.

Some people who have practiced the "TM technique" report that their perceptions have been sharpened?

Several perception tests have been made with TM students, and they have been invariably performed faster and more accurately. (The test consists of tracing complex patterns from their reflection in a mirror.) (19) In still another test, a group of meditators and a group of non-meditators were measured against each other for their ability to distinguish small differences in the length of auditory tones. Those who meditated with the "TM technique" showed more sensitive perceptions. (20)

Some people say that bronchial asthma is caused by the tensions in our minds. Is that true, and would meditating with the "TM technique" produce any improvement?

Asthma has long been thought to be a symptom of deep-set anxiety. After beginning to meditate with the "TM technique," 94 per cent of a group of asthmatics showed improvement according to the physiological measurements of airways resistance. Another survey showed that 61 per cent of the physicians involved felt their patients had improved. Of the patients themselves, 74 per cent said they felt there had been improvement in their condition. (21) (22) (23) (24)

Will the "TM technique" help me with any weight problems I may have?

If your weight problems are due to poor or excessive eating, the "TM technique" will not help you. What it will do is assist in stabilizing your metabolism. With your metabolism at a normal level your weight will begin to adjust itself to what it should be, barring glandular problems or continued excesses on your part. But if you practice a moderate diet and the "TM technique," you will have less problems with your weight.

Does meditation decrease a person's sensitivity to pain?

One of the most often noticed, and enigmatic, aspects of meditation is an insensitivity to pain. Perhaps the most investigated subject in this area has been Jack Schwarz, a forty-eight-year-old Dutchman who immigrated to the United States in 1957. In addition to sticking germatized needles through his arm without infection, Schwarz has placed burning cigarettes against his skin for periods of ten seconds. Instrumentation during these experiments with Dr. Elmer Green included a galvanic skin-reflex monitor which showed no noticeable increase in stress. The rate of Schwarz heart also increased by only a few beats during the needle experiments. Thermistors attached to the fingers revealed that his hand temperatures were high, a usual physiological sign of deep relaxation. During these experiments, Schwarz' brain wave patterns showed as much as 80 per cent alpha rhythms.

Dr. Elmer Green, of the Menninger Institute, recalls being worried during the first experiments not only by the apparent lack of pain but also the lack of bleeding. "So when I asked him if the wound was going to bleed and it did, I was more relieved than disappointed. This enabled me to see that there was nothing peculiar about his skin or blood, after all. By asking him whether there would be any bleeding I introduced a possibility that he had obviously shut out of his mind. This upset him a little; he went back into beta, and the bleeding began. Still, he demonstrated his control by stopping the bleeding instantly." (25)

Schwarz' own explanation is remarkably ingenuous. Pain, he says, is "man's servant . . . an alarm clock that wakes you when something goes wrong in the body that you should know about. But if you're doing something to the body of your own free will, something that you know is not really going to hurt you, then there is no reason for the alarm to go off, is there?"

To the author's knowledge, no research has been published concerning the effectiveness of the "TM technique" relative to pain insensitivity. It should be easy enough to measure, so perhaps such data will be forthcoming.

CHAPTER NINE

The Mental Benefits of Meditation

Does TM meditation enable a person to recover more quickly from stressful situations?

Absolutely. Not only do meditators perform better during moments of stress, but continued practice with the "TM technique" enables them to achieve a level of restful alertness at all times. Because of this factor, they are also able to recover more quickly from tense situations.

Tests in sleep deprivation, an experience which produces great stress, have shown that the recovery time for a group of meditators was much faster than that of non-meditators. Measurement was made in terms of dreaming, since dreaming is thought to be a form of release from tension. The nervous system of TM students becomes more resilient and less apt to undergo long-range after-effects as a result of tension.

101

What is meant by "restful alertness?"

"Restful alertness" is a phrase which TM meditators use to describe the "fourth state of consciousness" which the mind achieves during TM meditation. (The three traditional states are waking, dreaming, and sleeping.) The discovery of this "fourth state of consciousness" was made by Prof. Robert Keith Wallace, *et. al.,* in 1970. He found the with the practice of the TM technique, "there is a spreading of 8-9 cycles-per-second waves to the more frontal areas of the brain with the occasional occurrence of prominent and synchronized 5-7 cycles-per-second waves . . . these brain waves indicate a unique physiological state different from waking and sleeping—a state of alertness along with restfulness." (26) (27) (28) (29)

Is there any scientific proof that meditation will reduce anxiety and help us to increase our inner control?

We have already seen how the presence of lactate in the blood is one indicator of the stress level. Numerous other tests exist which measure anxiety. One is the Institute for Personality and Ability Testing Anxiety Scale (30), others are the Spielberger Anxiety inventory and the Cattell Anxiety Scale. (31) All have been used in testing anxiety in TM students, and without exception this group has registered less anxiety than non-meditators.

It has been consistently noted that anxiety levels are lower in long-term meditators, indicating that the benefits of the "TM technique" are cumulative.

Do meditators have faster reaction times than non-meditators?

An experiment conducted at the University of Texas by Robert Shaw and David Kolb indicates that meditators have substantially faster and more accurate reaction times than do non-meditators. They tested nine meditators and nine non-meditators—all average college students of about the same age. When asked to press a key on cue, meditators averaged a 30 per cent faster response than the non-meditators. This result may be attributed to the fact that the non-meditators became tense and feared they would not "succeed," while the meditating students remained in a state of "restful alertness."

Will practicing the TM method increase my intelligence?

No. What the TM technique *will* do in enhance the meditator's ability to realize the full potential of his intelligence. This will enable him to respond to situations more quickly, with greater understanding and imagination. But for all practical purposes, realizing one's potential can be considered as an increase in one's actual intelligence. (32) (33)

Does meditation with the "TM technique" increase one's ability to concentrate?

In almost every way, as demonstrated by three tests. The first (the latency of auto-kinetic effect test) measured the amount of time it took a subject to perceive the movement in a spot of light. The second test, the Rod-and-Frame, measured his ability to stand a rod vertically against a tilted frame. The final, Embedded-Figures Test, determined the subject's ability to distinguish simple figures camouflaged against an intricate background.

These tests indicate an improvement in both kinds of attention—broad and focused, without being distracted for longer periods of time than non-meditators. In addition, this improvement in adult meditators disproved the long standing belief that such neurological development in these basic perceptual abilities did not change beyond early adulthood. (34) (35)

Will I learn faster if I practice the "TM

technique?"

Definitely. Recall tests conducted between meditators and non-meditators showed a significantly better result for meditators, over both short-term and long-term recall tests. (36) (37)

During an experiment conducted by Elmer and Alyce Green with Swami Rama, Alyce Green softly recited a number of prepared, almost meaningless sentences, such as "It is raining today, but tomorrow the sun will shine." Swami Rama after a deep state of meditation could repeat 85 per cent of the sentences verbatim and paraphrase the remainder. Such an experiment tends to confirm the opinion of many psychologists that the human mind, like a perfect sponge, absorbs every impression, and that the problem of "learning" is really one of remembering what we have learned.

Will following the TM program improve my grades in school?

Students using the "TM technique" as a supplement to their normal study habits were found to have effected a generalized improvement in both the functioning of their minds and nervous systems, so that a great mental effectiveness resulted from the wholeness of their personalities.

Is there any evidence that people perform better on their jobs after they begin practicing the TM method?

One of the most investigated areas from which evidence has come to prove the effectiveness of the "TM technique" has been that of job performance. Tests have been conducted in terms of performance itself, productivity and job satisfaction. With better performance comes increased productivity and, with that, increased satisfaction with one's work. This improvement has been noticed on both an individual and an organizational basis. (38)

Will meditation bring any relief from chronic insomnia?

Since tension situations generally, and those connected with one's job in particular, are a major cause of insomnia, the "TM technique" was tested to see if any significant improvement resulted. As therapy, the "TM technique" relaxes and stabilizes the basic biological rhythms, so that subjects found immediately effective relief, and without any of the unfavorable side-effects of pills. (39) (40)

Furthermore, insomniacs as well as "normal sleepers" will be able to get along with less sleep as a result of meditating.

CHAPTER TEN

A Changing Life-Style?

Won't the "TM technique" require a change in my life?

Absolutely not! Beyond the time you give to the technique each morning and evening, you may carry on your life in your normal way. However, change from your old way of living *will* result, but it will not be required of you. It will come about naturally, almost without your noticing it. The continued practice of the "TM technique" always results in an eventual change in lifestyle. This change comes about because of the change which occurred in your mind. You will be much more relaxed, much more aware of life, filled with more energy, finding yourself thinking ideas which would never have occurred to you before, and more interested in other people's ideas. You will be much more open to all that is going on around you, able to absorb what is good from life and less susceptible to its negative influences.

Will I notice my personality change through meditation?

Your personality *will* change—and for the better. But there will probably be few changes, apart from feeling less tense, which you will notice yourself. A usual experience with meditators is that they become discouraged after three to six months (a really minimal time to produce any important change in oneself) because they feel "nothing is happening." Then one day someone will say to them, "You've really changed!" The personality changes which occur are very subtle—and they will be much more apparent to other people than they will be to you.

Since the "TM technique" doesn't vary from one person to another, won't it tend to make everyone the same?

This is one of the most widely held misconceptions about the "TM technique" and, oddly enough, it is the TM program which has fostered it. Patricia Drake Hemingway, herself a beneficiary of TM, comments upon TM classes: "Many of the young instructors of TM are rather lackluster. That is one of the few criticisms I have run across in the TM movement, the quality of the instructors. This is not only my observation but the complaint of many intelligent people who, for this reason, have not continued beyond the first or second advanced lecture. They say the teachers teach by rote; they answer questions by rote, like Bell Telephone operators are taught to do." (41)

The reason for this "dullness and uniformity" is because the spiritual leader of the TM movement, Maharishi Mahesh Yogi, does not want the teaching diluted by each teacher expressing himself in his or her own way, thus changing the original meaning.

The point is: the uniformity of the teaching does not affect the benefits of the "TM technique." Each meditator is a different person, and his *potentiality* is different. The "TM technique" enables each person to realize himself to the fullest extent. But just as no two people are going to be the same to begin with, no two people are going to be the same after they begin meditating.

Will using the TM technique make me more creative?

No, not if you mean will it give you artistic abilities which you don't already have. But it will enable you to make a more creative use of your own life. And that is an art, too.

The Torrence Test of Creative Thinking was developed to test the type of creative thinking described by scientists, inventors and writers. Psychologists Carl Rogers and Abraham Maslow have associated this test with an increase in self-realization. Both the results of this test and that prior are the natural effect of the mind being able, through the "TM technique," to directly experience the source of creativity which is in each of us.

Will meditation help one to cut down on such highly addictive drugs such as cigarettes and alcohol?

Meditation will not make you *want* to stop smoking and drinking; it will simply make it easier for you to do. Much of drinking and nearly all smoking is built not so much upon desire as upon need: the need of the smoker for nervous release, the need of the drinker to find temporary escape from the problems and tensions of his life. The continued practice of the "TM technique" brings, to both the mind and the body, a deep-seated relaxation. By resting the nervous system, the "TM technique" makes a person calmer, and by enhancing their creativity, reduces the frustration level. (42)

Has TM meditation been shown to have any effects on social situations—such as criminal rehabilitation?

Galvanic Skin Response tests given to prisoners before and after two months of TM practice, indicates the lowering of their stress levels. The meditating prisoners became more emotionally stable, better able to adapt to their new prison conditions, and began to participate more in positive activities such as sports, clubs, and utilizing educational opportunities. The integration of thinking and emotion necessary for true rehabilitation provides a basis for their later leading balanced and useful lives in society.

Results achieved with the Minnesota Multiphasic Personality Inventory (MMPI) corroborated the results given here and confirmed the value of the TM practice in the rehabilitation of criminals. (43) (44) (45) (48) (49).

Will meditation help to decrease the amount of prejudice in the world today?

A study conducted in a modern urban high school between students of widely different ethnic and social backgrounds showed an increase in tolerance levels as a result of TM practice. (46)

113

CHAPTER ELEVEN

The Experience of Meditation

What is the difference between the technique of meditation and the experience of meditation?

The "TM technique" results in meditation, but while the technique itself remains unchanged from the first session, the continuing experience of meditation provides the meditator with ceaseless opportunities for inner change and growth.

Then what are we conscious of when we practice the TM method of meditation?

We enter into a state of *pure consciousness*. Such is ultimately the goal of all forms of meditation. The "TM technique" simply enables us to achieve such a state more easily and more rapidly. As Harold Bloomfield and his co-authors so well express it: "When a meditator allows his attention to shift inward, he experiences quiet levels of the mind in which he becomes increasingly aware of the unbounded nature of his awareness in the absence of objects. This state . . . consists of nothing more than being wide awake inside without being aware of anything except awareness itself." (47)

Isn't the "TM technique," like other forms of meditation, based on foreign ways of thinking?

Not at all. Admittedly, the best known forms of meditation, at least in the Christian world, are Zen, yoga and Sufism; but that is probably because Christians know very little about their own systems of meditation. Evelyn Underhill, in her massive study of the subject, informs us that meditators and mystics have constituted: " . . . a curious and definite type of personality; a type which refuses to be satisfied with what other men call experience . . . We meet these persons in the east and the west; in the ancient, medieval, and modern worlds. Their one passion appears to be the prosecution of a certain spiritual . . . quest: the finding of a 'way out' or a 'way back' to some desirable state in which alone they can satisfy their craving for absolute truth. This quest, for them, has constituted the whole

118

meaning of life." (48)

Well, what is the connection then between "TM technique" and Zen, Sufism and especially yoga?

Despite the rivalries which exist between different schools of meditation, the aims, doctrines and methods of meditators over the ages have been remarkably self-consistent and often mutually explanatory. So before looking specifically at the connection between the TM method and other forms of meditation, let us take a look at those characteristics of the meditative experience which seem to be universal and familiar to all well-developed meditators. In this way we will see that despite the simplicity of the "TM technique," the experience of meditating by this means is a highly complex one.

(1) Meditation presumes a reality which lies beyond the world of the senses and the merely rational mind.

(2) The meditator realizes, therefore, that this reality cannot be found by rational theorizing upon sense data but only by a practical method of proceeding through some channel other than reason and the senses. A way which provides direct contact with this inner realm must be developed.

(3) The meditator asserts that he can

experience the ultimate reality for man by a contact so intense as to constitute a union. He feels that he has discovered himself to be merged with, and a part of, this ultimate reality.

(4) The meditator believes that mere hallucination and the reality of his experience can be distinguished. He does not attribute his experience to illusion, subjectivity, overexcitement of the brain, or neural damage, but that this experience provides him with the knowledge of spiritual realities that lie beyond mere sense experience.

(5) Meditation usually involves an intense spiritual pilgrimage by the meditator before he is able to attain that state of passivity in which the breakthrough occurs. Meditation requires a movement of the mind from activity to passivity before union with reality can be experienced.

(6) The meditator's motivation is not a coolly rational one that wishes to examine reality at a distance. His aim is not to know *about* reality, but to *know* reality. The necessary activity which precedes the passive state is one of great longing for reality.

(7) The meditator believes that such longing forces him to proceed patiently, opening up his direct channels to ultimate reality in a disciplined way.

(8) The meditator finds that this experience reveals to him that all things exist in

essential harmony. Man and his universe are one and yet many; they are many and yet one.

(9) The meditator finds that his experience of union with reality brings with it a sense of the sacredness of all life because he is at peace with himself. His sense of awe and reverence for life are stirred.

(10) The meditator discovers a great change has been produced in him. His values have been transcended. Much of what he formerly thought real, he now considers unreal; much of what he once valued, he now no longer thinks about at all.

(11) Because his experience of union has been so profound, so overwhelming and energizing, his response is one of newfound joy in living and an outpouring of energies he had not realized he had. His previous negative attitudes gone, new powers for living are tapped, including a sense of humor at the seriousness with which other people continue to take themselves.

(12) Since the meditator feels that he is at One with all things, and all things are in a sense One with him, he develops a desire to live life more sacrificially and lovingly. Just as the ultimate reality is a creating and caring for all things, so the meditator, having experienced it, wishes to live in its essence, creating a fuller life for others and

caring for them in it.

(13) Some changes in our consciousness, such as occur with the use of drugs, can become permanent. But the meditator realizes that the highest moments of meditation flash and are gone. He realizes, too, that while the experience is transient, the effects of it are not.

(14) With disappointment, the meditator realizes that his experience is beyond description, that it is so different from the world of the senses that he cannot share it with non-meditators. They cannot quite imagine what he has experienced.

(15) Since his experience is beyond ordinary description, the meditator must often resort to paradox and poetic language in his efforts to describe the unnamable. The ultimate reality which he has touched, for example, is described as the Filled Abyss, the Everything in Nothing, the Dark Light, and, very commonly, the union of the meditator and reality is described as a love affair between a man and a woman.

Will there be future discouragement with the TM technique?

With every not yet mature meditator, there will be frequently recurring periods of mental stagnation. Such moments are usually the result of the meditator having over-extended himself or of meditating incorrectly. There is a period of adolescence in meditation, which lasts until the meditator establishes a state of balance between his life and the new experience which has entered into it.

What is this state of balance and how does one achieve it?

The final stage is called the "Unitive Life." It means that the higher consciousness achieved during meditation has established itself as the governing force in one's life. With repeated practice, we remake, transform and unify our selves and our lives. With all tensions now gone from the mind, all stress from the body, we have liberated an enormous amount of energy which must now be put to some practical purpose.

Why do we seem to rely so much on the evidence of our bodies to tell us what is going on in our minds while we are meditating?

Largely because of the meditators themselves. As the research of Dr. Joseph Kamiya and others has shown, verbal descriptions of "what happens" during meditation, like those of mystical enlightenment, have proven to be often contradictory or vague. When Dr. Bernard Engel, a psychologist in Baltimore City Hospital, asked his subjects about the mind-body control which meditation produces, one woman replied she imagined herself in a swing, another thought about running down a dark street.

The meditative experience is essentially ineffable, or beyond verbal description. Despite the widespread use and ease of learning the "TM technique," the mind appears at a loss to explain its own workings. Subjects report a variety of emotional and pictorial responses during meditation, and the researcher can safely conclude only that meditators know they *can* achieve results, but beyond a certain point, they do not know *how* they achieve them.

Why is the meditative state so elusive, so difficult to describe, even after we have experienced it?

There have been a lot of answers to that question, but all we know for sure is that it seems to be a fact of life. One of the more interesting answers is that given by Professor Brown, in the *Laws of Form*. He expresses the view that our universe seems to be "constructed in order (and thus in such a way as to be able) to see itself. But in order to do so, evidently it must first cut itself up into at least one *state which sees* and at least one *state which is seen*. In this severed and mutilated condition, whatever it sees is only partially itself . . . but in any attempt to see itself, as an object, it must equally undoubtedly, act so as to make itself distinct from, and therefore false to, itself. In this condition, it will always partially elude itself." (49)

What does the meditation experience feel like?

Traditionally, mystics and meditators have tried to express the "sense of oneness" which they feel by appealing to parallels between this world and their experience of unity with themselves, the Godhead, the Absolute, or call it what you will. Writing within a religious context, Jakob Boehme has probably offered as good a description as anyone: "Behold a bright, flaming piece of iron, which of itself is dark and black, and the fire so penetrateth and shineth through the iron that it giveth light. Now the iron does not *cease to be*; it is iron still; and the source (or property) of the fire retaineth its own property; it doth not take the iron into it, but penetrateth (and shineth) through the iron; and it is iron then as well as before, *free* in itself; and so also is the source or property of the *fire*. In such a manner is the soul set in the Deity; the Deity penetrateth the soul, and dwelleth in the soul, yet the soul doth not comprehend the Deity, but the Deity comprehendeth the soul, but doth not alter it (from being a soul) but only giveth it the divine source (or property) of the majesty." (50)

It requires a great deal of imagination to understand this answer, but it is one of the better descriptions we have of the meditative state. Most readers will not be content with such descriptions; they will find it easier to answer the question for themselves— by beginning to practice meditation.

ACKNOWLEDGEMENTS

Numerous people have given me aid in the course of writing this book. I should very much like to thank all of the people, firms, and institutions that aided my endeavors, most notably Mr. Martin Ebon and Mr. Raymond Van Over, whose conversation, advice and patience, as always, have been invaluable. I am grateful also to those friends who read and criticized this manuscript during the early stages. Thanks are also due to Canon William V. Rauscher and. Canon Robert Lewis, whose private libraries have proven invaluable over the years. I am also endebted to Mrs. Ellyn Childs Allison for her quick responses to my appeals for help. Most of all, however, I owe a debt of gratitude to my publishers, Sidney and Russell Mehlman, who have been not only my good advisors and critics, but without whose encouragement and patience, this book could not have been brought to completion.

NOTES

1. Charles Keen: "The Soft Revolution, " (*The Christian Century,* Dec. 31, 1969), p. 1667.
2. Lewis Mumford: *The Making of a Counter Culture.* (New York: Doubleday and Co., 1969), pp. 62-63.
3. *The Autobiography of St. Therese of Lisieux*, trans. J Beevers. (New York: Doubleday Image, 1973), p. 133.
4. Harold Bloomfield, *et. al.: TM, Discovering Inner Energy and Overcoming Stress.* (New York: Delacorte, 1975), pp. 20-21.
5. Leon S. Otis in "Right Now," (*McCall's*, Jan., 1976), p. 46.
6. Herbert Benson: *The Relaxation Response.* (New York: William Morrow and Co., 1975), p. 18.
7. Herbert Benson; *op. cit.*, p. 115.
8. Herbert Benson; *op. cit.*, pp. 113-114.
9. Robert Keith Wallace and Herbert Benson: "The Physiology of Meditation," (*Scientific American*, Feb., 1972), p. 87.
10. Tom J. Routt: "Low Normal Heart and Respiratory Rates in Practitioners of Transcendental Meditation,"

(Huxley College of Environmental Studies, Western Washington State University, Bellingham, 1973).

11. Robert Keith Wallace: "The Physiological Effects of Transcendental Meditation: A proposed Fourth Major State of Consciousness," (Ph.D. Thesis, Department of Physiology, University of California, Los Angeles, 1970).

12. Bernard Law Collier: "Brain Power" (*Saturday Review*, Apr. 10, 1971), pp. 11-12.

13. Benson: *The Relaxation Response*, p. 38.

14. Herbert Benson and Robert Keith Wallace: "Decreased Blood Pressure in Hypertensive Subjects Who Practiced Meditation," (*Circulation*, 45 and 46, Supplement II, 1972).

15. Barry Blackwell, *et. al.:* "Effects of Transcendental Meditation on Blood Pressure; A Controlled Pilot Experiment," *(Journal of Psychosomatic Medicine;* vol. 37, 1975), p. 86.

16. Wallace and Benson; *Scientific American*, p. 87.

17. F.N. Pitts, Jr. and J.N. McClure, Jr.: "Lactate Metabolism in Anxiety Neurosis," (*New England Journal of Medicine,* Vol. 277, (1967), pp.

1329-1336.

18.   Wallace and Benson; *Scientific American*, p. 87.

19.   Karen Blasdell: "The Effects of Transcendental Meditation Upon a Complex Perceptual-Motor Task," in *Scientific Research on Transcendental Meditation: Collected Papers,* Vol. 1, ed. David W. Orme-Johnson, *et. al.* (Los Angeles: MIU Press, 1974.)

20.   Michael Pirot: "Transcendental Meditation and Perceptual Auditory Discrimination," (Department of Psychology, University of Victoria, Victoria, British Columbia, Canada, 1973).

21.   Ron Honsberger and Archie F. Wilson: "Transcendental Meditation in Treating Asthma," (*Respiratory Therapy: The Journal of Inhalation Technology*; Vol. 3, No. 6; 1973), pp. 79-81.

22.   Ron Honsberger and Archie F. Wilson: "The Effects of Transcendental Meditation upon Bronchial Asthma," (*Clinical Research;.*Vol. 2, No. 2; 1973).

23.   Archie F. Wilson, Ron Honsberger, *et. al.:* "Transcendental Meditation and Asthma," (*Respiration*; Vol. 32;

1973), pp. 74-80.

24.   Paul W. Corey: "Airway Conductance and Oxygen Consumption Changes Associated with Practice of the Transcendental Meditation Technique," (University of Colorado Medical Center; Denver, Colorado).

25.   David M. Rorvik: "Jack Schwarz Feels No Pain," (*Esquire*, Dec., 1972), p. 210.

26.   Robert Keith Wallace: "The Physiological Effects of Transcendental Meditation: a Proposed Fourth Major State of Consciousness," (Ph.D. Thesis, Department of Physiology, University of California, Los Angeles, 1970).

27.   Robert Keith Wallace, Herbert Benson and Archie F. Wilson: "A Wakeful Hypometabolic Physiologic State," (*American Journal Of Physiology;* Vol. 221, No. 3; 1971), pp. 795-799.

28.   Robert Keith Wallace and Herbert Benson; *Scientific American*, pp. 84-90.

29.   Jean-Paul Banquet and Maurice Sailhan: "Analyse E.E.G. d'etats de conscience induits et spontanes," (*(Revue D'Electroencephalographie et Neurophysiologie;* Vol. 4; France,

1974), pp. 445-453.

30. Lawrence Farwell: "Effect of Transcendental Meditation on Level of Anxiety," in *Scientific Research on Transcendental Meditation: Collected Papers,* Vol. 1, ed. David W. Orme-Johnson, *et. al.* (Los Angeles: MIU Press, 1974.)

31. Philip C. Ferguson and John C. Gowan: "The Influence of Transcendental Meditation on Anxiety, Depression, Aggression, Neuroticism and Self-Actualization," (Paper presented at California State Psychological Association, Fresno, California, 1974).

32 Andre S. Tjoa: "Some Evidence that. the Transcendental Meditation Program Increases Intelligence and Reduces Neuroticism as Measured by Psychological Tests," (University of Leiden, Leiden, the Netherlands).

33. Andre S. Tjoa: "Meditation, Neuroticism and Intelligence; A Follow Up," (*Gedrag. Tijdschrift voor Psychologie,* Vol. 3, the Netherlands, 1975), pp. 167-182.

34. Kenneth R. Pelletier: "The Effects of the Transcendental Meditation Program on Perceptual Style; Increased Field Independence," (University of

California School of Medicine, San
Francisco).

35. Kenneth R. Pelletier: "Influence of
Transcendental Meditation upon
Autokinetic Perception," (*Perceptual and Motor Skills*; Vol. 39; 1974),
pp. 1031-1034.

36. Allen I. Abrams: "Paired-Associate
Learning and Recall: A Pilot Study
of the Transcendental Meditation
Technique," (University of California, Berkeley).

37. Donald E. Miskiman: "Performance
in a Learning Task by Subjects Who
Practice the Transcendental Meditation Technique," (Univeristy of
Alberta, Edmonton, Alberta,
Canada).

38. David R. Frew: "Transcendental
Meditation and Productivity,"
Academy of Management Journal;
Vol. 17, No. 2; 1974), pp. 362-368.

39. Donald E. Miskiman: "The Treatment of Insomnia by Transcendental
Meditation Technique," *Scientific
Research on Transcendental Meditation: Collected Papers,* Vol. 1, eds.
David W. Orme-Johnson, *et. al.* (Los
Angeles: MIU Press, 1974).

40. Donald E. Miskiman: "Long-Term
Effects of the Transcendental Medi-

tation Technique on the Treatment of Insomnia," (University of Alberta, Edmonton, Alberta, Canada).

41. Patricia Drake Hemingway: *The Transcendental Meditation Primer.* (New York: David McKay and Co., 1975), pp. 37-38.

42. Herbert Benson and Robert Keith Wallace: "Decreased Drug Abuse with Transcendental Meditation; A Study of 1,862 Subjects," *Drug Abuse: Proceedings of the International Conference,* ed. Chris J.D. Zarafonetis. (Philadelphia: Lea and Febiger, 1972), pp. 369-376.

43. David W. Orme-Johnson, *et. al.*: "Personality and Autonomic Changes in Meditating Prisoners," (La Tuna Penitentiary, New Mexico, 1972).

44. David Ballou: "Transcendental Meditation at Stillwater Prison," (Department of Anthropology, Kansas University, Lawrence, Kansas, 1974).

45. Monte Cunningham and Walter Koch: "A Pilot Project at the Federal Correctional Institute at Lompoc, California," *Scientific Research on Transcendental Meditation: Collected Papers*, Vol. 1, ed. David W. Orme-Johnson, *et. al.* (Los Angeles;

MIU Press, 1974).

46. Howard Shecter: "The Transcendental Meditation Program in the Classroom: A Psychological Evaluation," (York University, North York, Ontario, Canada).

47. Harold Bloomfield, *et. al.; op. cit.,* p. 11.

48. Evelyn Underhill: *Mysticism.* (New York: Dutton and Co., 1961), p. 3.

49. G. Brown: *Laws of Form.* (London: Allen, 1969), p. 105.

50. Jakob Boehme: *The Threefold Life of Man.* (London: Allen, 1909), Chap. vi, p. 88.

BIOGRAPHICAL NOTE

W.R. AKINS began the study of Zen meditation and Chinese mysticism while in college. Since that time, he has continued to meditate and has become familiar with most meditative techniques, both Eastern and Western. Most recently, he has become a student of Transcendental Meditation.

Formerly Executive Director of the Parapsychology Foundation, and Editor of its *Journal* and *Newsletter,* Mr. Akins was for several years Editor of the *Journal* of the Spiritual Frontiers Society, a group devoted to the study of meditation and prayer. He is the author of *New Worlds, New Anatomies,* a study of meditation and the creative process, and the *Encyclopedia of Psychic and Occult Studies* (forthcoming; David McKay). Presently, he is at work on a new book, *Basic Meditation Techniques.*

H. GEORGE NURNBERG, M.D., is Assistant Professor of Psychiatry at the New York Hospital-Cornell Medical Center. Dr. Nurnberg has practiced psychiatry and psychoanalysis in New York City and has had a longstanding interest in the use of relaxation techniques and meditation in the treatment of emotional disorders.